D0498082

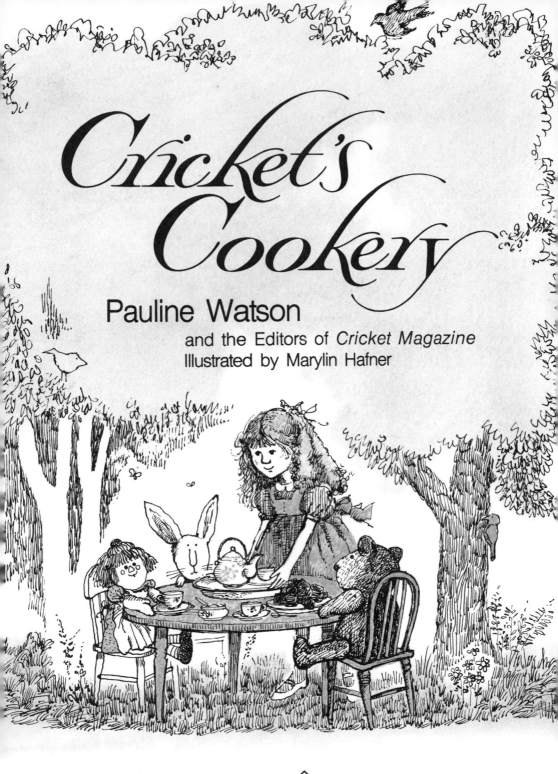

Cricket's Cookery

Pauline Watson
and the Editors of *Cricket Magazine*
Illustrated by Marylin Hafner

Random House New York

Copyright © 1977 by Random House, Inc., and Open Court Publishing Company.
All rights reserved under International and Pan-American Copyright
Conventions. Published in the United States by Random House, Inc., New York,
and simultaneously in Canada by Random House of Canada Limited, Toronto.

LIBRARY OF CONGRESS CATALOGING IN PUBLICATION DATA

Watson, Pauline.   Cricket's Cookery.   SUMMARY: Presents twenty-eight
simple recipes, with most set to the tunes of familiar songs. Grand Slam Chicken
is cooked to the tune of Take Me Out to the Ball Game.   1. Cookery—Juvenile
literature.   [1. Cookery]   I. Hafner, Marylin.   II. Cricket.   III. Title.
IV. Title: Cookery.   TX652.5.W37   641.5   77-3637   ISBN: 0-394-83540-9
ISBN: 0-394-93540-3 (lib. bdg.)

Manufactured in the United States of America   1 2 3 4 5 6 7 8 9 0

Contents

Here are some of the utensils you will use in this book:

pot holders

3-quart pot with lid

skillet with lid

1-quart saucepan

colander

measuring cups

for dry ingredients

Tools of the Trade

chopping board

1-quart casserole dish

mixing bowls

pie pans

(8-inch and 9-inch)

griddle

cookie sheet

measuring cup for liquids

square cake pans (8-inch and 9-inch)

What's Cooking?

Here is a funny game for you to play. Read each question and circle the correct answer.

1. Before you start cooking, it is important to ask the permission of:
   a. a hungry pet   b. the top chef of the household   c. the weather bureau
2. When you have decided which dish to prepare, read the recipe:
   a. while standing on your head   b. 184 times
   c. straight through, once
3. The ingredients and utensils you will need should be:
   a. gathered together and set out near you before you begin   b. borrowed from the neighbors   c. left on the shelf
4. The best thing to wear while cooking is:
   a. a wig   b. an apron   c. a raincoat
5. If you do not know how to use the stove or peel a potato or grease a pan, you should:
   a. call it dumb and kick it   b. ask an adult to teach you   c. dial information

6. The safest way to chop a vegetable is:
   a. on a chopping board with the knife-tip away from you   b. in your hand with the knife toward you   c. with an ax
7. When you preheat the oven you:
   a. place hot peppers in it   b. turn it on before you mix the ingredients   c. turn on the kitchen light
8. When greasing a pan, spread oil:
   a. by wiggling the pan   b. with your nose   c. using a small piece of paper towel
9. To measure one cup of flour accurately:
   a. jiggle the measuring cup to settle the flour   b. form a mountain peak of flour   c. fill the cup and level it with a knife
10. A "pinch" is:
   a. something you give your little brother   b. a very small quantity of an ingredient   c. a tight shoe
11. "Sauté" means:
   a. fry quickly in a little fat   b. add salt and pepper   c. boil some water
12. "Cream the shortening" means:
   a. stir it with a spoon until it's soft and fluffy   b. pour cream over it   c. melt it in the sun
13. Unless the recipe says otherwise, the oven rack should be placed:
   a. in the center of the oven   b. on top of Old Smokey   c. on the bottom of the oven
14. "Simmer" means:
   a. cook two weeks   b. remove from heat   c. cook slowly in liquid over low heat

15. When removing a pan from the stove top or oven, use:
a. bare hands b. pot holders c. velvet mittens
16. Good cooks:
a. forget to turn off the oven b. leave the kitchen in a mess c. willingly wash hands and pans, put everything back in order, and sweep the kitchen

Answers to
What's Cooking?

1. b
2. c
3. a
4. b
5. b
6. a
7. b
8. c
9. c
10. b
11. a
12. a
13. a
14. c
15. b
16. c

Disappearing Toast

A fresh slice of bread that I know
Was buttered from head down to toe.
It was dotted with jelly
All over its belly.
It was baked—now it's gone—where'd it go?

To solve the mystery, you will need these facts: A fresh slice of bread was spread with 1 teaspoon soft butter and dotted with 1/2 teaspoon jelly. It was placed on a cookie sheet and baked in a 350 degree oven for 7 minutes.

Clues to remember: As soon as the toast was removed from the oven, it disappeared. One glass of milk vanished, too. The only one in the kitchen was the cook. What happened to the toast?

Can you solve this mystery?

Scrambled Eggs

You will need: small mixing bowl, measuring spoons, fork, skillet.

Ingredients:

2 eggs
4 quick shakes salt
1 pinch pepper
2 tablespoons milk
1 tablespoon butter
bacon bits

Put eggs, salt, pepper, and milk
Into a mixing bowl.
Beat with a fork and mix a bit;
Keep eggs under control.

Melt butter in skillet on stove.
Tilt skillet; let butter ramble.
Pour in eggs and lower heat;
Stir eggs with fork, and scramble.

Have toast all buttered and waiting on a warm plate. Place scrambled eggs on the plate, sprinkle with bacon bits, and serve at once with a cold glass of milk.

Serves 1 hungry tummy.

Preheat oven to 300 degrees.

You will need: measuring cups, measuring spoons, small bowl, stirring spoon, spatula, lightly greased griddle, waxed paper, toothpicks.

Ingredients:

3/4 cup flour
1/2 teaspoon salt
1 teaspoon baking powder
1 egg
3/4 cup milk (remove 1 tablespoon of milk if the egg is large)
1 teaspoon cooking oil
soft butter
cinnamon sugar

14

Mix to the tune of *Alouette*.

Measure flour, salt, and baking powder.
Put them all into a bowl and stir.
Next, put milk and egg in bowl;
Then put cooking oil in bowl.
Milk and egg! Cooking oil!
Milk and egg! Cooking oil!
O-o-o-oh, stir and blend well; spoon onto hot griddle.
Don't forget to flip them over once.

Place each pancake on waxed paper, Spread with soft butter and sprinkle with cinnamon sugar. Roll each pancake and secure with toothpick. (Keep pancakes warm in oven until all are ready to be served.) Serve hot.

Makes 12 pancakes.

Friendship Soup

You will need: 3-quart soup pot with lid, stirring spoon, potato peeler, paring knife, measuring cup, measuring spoons.

Ingredients:

2 carrots, washed and sliced
1 stalk celery, chopped
1 small onion, peeled and chopped
2 stems of parsley, chopped
2 medium potatoes, peeled and chopped
1 cup canned tomatoes
3 cups water
2 bouillon cubes
3/4 teaspoon salt
2 wieners, sliced

Mix to the tune of *When the Saints Come Marching In.*

Put everything (Put everything)
Into the pot. (Into the pot.)
Put everything into the pot. (Yes-sir-ree!)
Then let it cook and go dial a number.
Ask two friends to drop in, please. (Yes, indeed!)

Now stir the soup; (Now stir the soup;)
Turn heat down low. (Turn heat down low.)
Now stir the soup; turn heat down low. (*Friendship Soup!*)
Oh, let it simmer, oh, let it slumber—
Till your friends come marching in.

Or about 1 hour. Makes 5 cups. Serve with crackers.

You will need: 1-quart saucepan, slotted spoon, measuring cup, 2 bowls, measuring spoons, stirring spoon, fork, teaspoon, paring knife.

Ingredients:

3 eggs
2 cups cold water
1 teaspoon vinegar
1 tablespoon prepared mustard
1 tablespoon French dressing
1 tablespoon dill pickle, finely chopped
1 teaspoon pickle juice

Place the eggs in the saucepan. Cover with water and add vinegar. Bring water to a boil; turn heat down low and simmer for 20 minutes.

While the eggs are cooking, mix the remaining ingredients in a small bowl.

When the eggs are done, remove them from the saucepan with the slotted spoon and place them in a bowl of cold water. When they are cool, shell the eggs and cut them in half lengthwise. Remove the yellow yolks with a teaspoon and put them into a bowl with the sauce mixture.

Prepare to the tune of *This Old Man.*

Boil the eggs till they're done;
Cool and shell and half each one.
With a nick-nack, tangy snack, give the dog a bone,
But save these eggs for me alone.

In the sauce mash the yolks;
Mash and mix with lively strokes.
With a nick-nack, tangy snack, give the dog a bone.
Spoon each deviled egg yolk home.

Makes enough for you and two devilish friends.

Ya-Hoo Salad

You will need: 9-inch pie pan, stirring spoon, measuring cup, saucepan.

Ingredients:

1 (3-oz.) package lemon-flavored gelatin
1 1/4 cups water
1 cup canned crushed pineapple
lettuce, rinsed in cold water
5 cherries

Heat water in saucepan until it boils; then pour it into the pie pan.

Stir gelatin into hot water. Ya-hoo!
(Keep fingers away from the steam as you do.)
Set pan in the icebox and chill through and through.
An hour, and it will be wiggle-de-goo.

Add pineapple to it and stir it. Ya-hoo!
Put back into icebox and say, "Toodle-ooo!"
When firm, place on lettuce and serve to a few.
As soon as they taste it, they'll be proud of you!

Top each salad with a bright red cherry. Serves 5.

Oh, Banana Bread!

Preheat oven to 350 degrees.

You will need: large bowl, fork, stirring spoon, measuring spoons, measuring cups, greased 8-inch square cake pan.

Ingredients:

2 ripe bananas, mashed
2 eggs
1 cup sugar
1/2 cup cooking oil
1 teaspoon baking soda
2 cups flour
1/2 teaspoon salt
1/2 cup pecans, chopped

21

Mix to the tune of *Oh, Susanna!*

I'm mashing the bananas and I'm having lots of fun;
I'm adding eggs and sugar now, to make the mixture one.
Oh, banana! Oh, bread, you're good to eat!
But I have to whip your batter, so forgive me while I beat.

I'm going to add the cooking oil, the soda, flour, salt;
I'm stirring in the nuts so that the bread will have no fault.
Oh, banana! Oh, bread, I must repeat:
I will have to whip your batter, so forgive me while I beat.

I'm pouring you into a pan to bake you golden brown,
And in an hour you will be the best fruit bread in town.
Oh, banana! Oh, bread, I do love you.
I will eat you when you're ready, so forgive me while I chew.

Bake banana bread 1 hour.
Makes 16 2-inch squares.

I went to a fancy food fair;
A prize-winning chef was there.
And he said to me,
"Here's a rare recipe.
Try cooking it if you dare."

Absent-Minded Pudding

Preheat oven to 325 degrees.

You will need: measuring cups, measuring spoons, stirring spoon, bowl, 1-quart buttered casserole dish.

Absent-Minded Ingredients:

1 cup what-cha-ma-call-it
1 cup doodle-ma-jiggies
1 what's-its-face
1/4 cup thing-a-ma-jig
1/4 teaspoon sprinkly-stuff
1/2 teaspoon uh-uh
1/2 cup do-dads
1/2 teaspoon you-know

In a bowl, pour the what-cha-ma-call-it over the doodle-ma-jiggies and let stand for 5 minutes. Add the what's-its-face, the thing-a-ma-jig, the sprinkly-stuff, and the uh-uh. After that, add the do-dads and you-know. Mix well and pour into a buttered gizmo. Bake 40 minutes.

Serve with a squeeze of lemon and a dab of applesauce. Makes 4 servings.

What-cha-ma-call-it = evaporated milk. Doodle-ma-jiggies = day-old bread cubes. What's-its-face = egg. Thing-a-ma-jig = sugar. Sprinkly-stuff = salt. Uh-uh = cinnamon. Do-dads = raisins. You-know = vanilla. Gizmo = casserole dish.

Harvest Corn

You will need: paring knife, measuring spoons, stirring spoon, skillet with lid.

Ingredients:

3 ears of corn (cut corn off cob)
or 1 (12-oz.) can whole kernel corn, drained
1 tablespoon onion, chopped
1 tablespoon green pepper, chopped
1 heaping teaspoon bacon grease
1 (8-oz.) can tomato sauce
salt and pepper

Cook onion in grease;
Add green pepper, please.
Add corn off the ear
(or use canned corn, dear).
Salt and pepper to taste
(just a pinch, please, no waste).
Add tomato sauce now;
Stir, cook covered, WOW!

Simmer on low heat 30 minutes for fresh corn, 15 minutes for canned corn. Serves 4.

Baked Potatoes

Preheat oven to 500 degrees.

You will need: vegetable brush, towel, fork, long-handled fork, paring knife, skillet, stirring spoon.

Ingredients:

4 baking potatoes
vegetable oil or bacon drippings
1/2 stick oleomargarine
parsley flakes
seasoned salt

Give the potatoes a nice bath in cool water. Scrub each one well with a vegetable brush; then pat dry with a clean kitchen towel.

Give each potato a nice oil rubbing. Pour two drops of vegetable oil or bacon drippings over each one and rub well.

Prick the potatoes several times with a fork. This allows the steam to escape while they bake. Place the potatoes in the oven and bake at 500 degrees for 1 hour.

I am a BUTTER FLY!

While the potatoes are baking, melt 1/2 stick of margarine in a skillet. Turn the heat very low and add 4 shakes of parsley flakes and 2 shakes of seasoned salt to the melted margarine. Stir once, remove from the heat, and turn off the burner. Keep the skillet on the warm stove.

The potatoes are done when a fork goes into them easily. Turn off the oven and remove the potatoes with the long-handled fork. OOPS! There goes one onto the floor. Pick it up with a pot holder and dust it off.

Split the potatoes across the top with a sharp knife. Scrunch the two ends of each potato toward the middle. This makes them open like flowers in bloom. Pour a spoonful of the margarine mixture into every blooming one and serve at once.

Grand Slam Chicken

You will need: paper towel, skillet with lid, measuring spoons, measuring cups, chopping knife, long-handled fork.

Ingredients:

4 chicken drumsticks
1/2 cup flour
1/2 teaspoon salt
2 tablespoons vegetable oil
1/2 cup onions, chopped
1 cup hot water
1 chicken bouillon cube
1/2 teaspoon paprika

Add bouillon cube to hot water and set aside for broth.

Cook to the tune of *Take Me Out to the Ball Game.*

Rinse 4 drumsticks and pat dry;
Roll in flour and salt.
Place in a skillet with heated oil;
Brown a bit—keep an eye on your toil.
Pitch in onions, broth, and please throw straight—
To miss the pan is a shame.
For it's Pitch! Hit! Cover and cook!
For this grand slam game.

Simmer 1 hour. Sprinkle the four baseball bats with paprika. Serve on home plate with 4 olive balls.

Yankee Doodle Noodles

Preheat oven to 350 degrees.

You will need: 3-quart pot, measuring cups, measuring spoons, stirring spoon, colander, cheese grater, casserole dish. (To drain cooked noodles, put colander in sink. Using potholders, pour in noodles.)

Ingredients for noodles:

6 cups water
1 teaspoon salt
2 cups noodles

Ingredients for sauce:

4 tablespoons soft butter
1/4 cup milk
1 cup Cheddar cheese, grated
1/2 teaspoon salt

Ingredients for topping:

4 crackers, crumbled

Cook to the tune of *Yankee Doodle.*

32

Heat the water till it boils;
Now throw in salt and noodles.
Lower heat and stir and cook
Till noodles grow to oodles.

Drain and butter; place in dish
Yankee Doodle Noodles.
Stir in milk and cheese and salt,
And top with cracker-doodles.

Bake 20 minutes.
Serves 6.

Bravo Bean Bake

Preheat oven to 350 degrees.

You will need: cheese grater, chopping knife, measuring cups, measuring spoons, small buttered casserole dish, stirring spoon.

Ingredients:

1 cup cooked green beans
2 tablespoons canned cream of mushroom soup
2 tablespoons water
2 tablespoons green onion, chopped
1/4 cup sharp Cheddar cheese, grated

CHEF BRAVO: Dear tender Greenbeans, let me put you into this nice cozy casserole.

GREENBEANS: Plop!

CHEF BRAVO: You're next, Mushroom Soup.

SOUP: Sloop! Sloop!

CHEF BRAVO: Greenbeans, here come two sips of Water. Onions, too.

WATER: Splish! Splash!

ONIONS: Pat-pat.

CHEF BRAVO: Dear Greenbeans, I will stir you gently because I love you.

SPOON: Splink! Splonk! Splurrp!

CHEF BRAVO (looking surprised):   Oh, Cheese! There you are! It is time to sprinkle you over Greenbeans, isn't it?

CHEESE: Pitty-pat, pitty-pat, pitty-pat.

CHEF BRAVO (putting casserole in oven):   Farewell, my dear. I will see you again in 20 minutes.

Intermission

CHEF BRAVO (removing casserole from oven):   Hello, dear Greenbeans. 3 servings, you say? Mmmm . . . . In that case, I will be my own guest—TWICE!

The End

BRAVO

Mighty Meatballs

Preheat oven to 350 degrees.

You will need: casserole dish, stirring spoon, measuring spoons, bowl, clean hands.

Ingredients for sauce:

1 can tomato soup
1 can water
2 tablespoons brown sugar
4 whole cloves
1/2 teaspoon cinnamon

Ingredients for meatballs:

1 pound hamburger
1 tablespoon onion flakes
1 teaspoon salt
1/2 teaspoon cracked pepper
1 tablespoon peanut butter

Mix to the tune of *The Marine's Hymn.*

Empty can of soup in casserole;
Pour in can of water, please.
Stir in sugar, cloves, and cinnamon;
Leave the sauce to stand at ease.

Mix up hamburger with onion, salt;
Now please add the pepper grounds.
Work in peanut butter with your hands;
Roll into firm meatball rounds.

Place meatballs into sauce in casserole, cover, and bake 1 hour. Serve with cooked noodles to 6 mighty eaters.

You will need: chopping knife, potato peeler, measuring spoons, measuring cups, stirring spoon, small skillet with lid.

Ingredients:

1 tablespoon green onions, chopped
1 cup raw potatoes, peeled and cubed
1 teaspoon cooking oil
1/2 teaspoon salt
1/4 teaspoon paprika
1 cup beef bouillon (mix 1 cup hot water with 1 bouillon cube)

Cook to the tune of *I've Been Working on the Railroad*.

Brown the onion and potatoes—in the cooking oil.
Add the seasoning and the bouillon. Bring it to a boil.
Turn down heat and let it simmer—twenty minutes should be fine.
Don't you know that when it's ready, you'll be set to dine.

So, share it with a chum, share it with a chum,
Share it with a chum, your *Yum-Yum Stew.*
Share it with a chum, share it with a chum,
'Cause sharing's fun to do.

To thicken stew before sharing, mix 1 tablespoon flour
with 1/4 cup cold water, stir well, and pour into stew. Stir and
simmer 2 minutes longer. YUM! Serves 2.

Preheat oven to 350 degrees.

You will need: 8-inch pie pan, measuring cups, measuring spoons, fork.

Ingredients:

1 tablespoon flour
1/2 cup cold milk
1 (6 1/2-oz.) can tuna, drained
1/2 cup peas, drained

    This takes very little time to make, so read the recipe quickly, too. Ready?

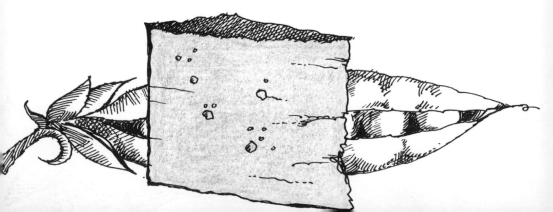

Put the flour in a cup
Add cold milk and stir it up
Scoop the tuna from the can
Spread it neatly in the pan
Sprinkle peas for tuna's hat
Pour milk mixture over that!

If you have 1 tablespoon chopped onion to stir into tuna, name the dish: Onion Tuna Pea Pie.

If you have 1/4 cup grated cheese to sprinkle over the top before baking, name the dish: Cheesy Onion Tuna Pea Pie.

If you serve it on a bun, name the dish: Cheesy Onion Tuna Pea Pie on a Bun.

Bake for 20 minutes. Serves 4 people with one bite left over for the cat.

Nutty Chocolate Cookies

Preheat oven to 375 degrees.

You will need: bowl, stirring spoon, greased cookie sheet, measuring cups, measuring spoons, teaspoon.

Ingredients:

1/2 cup shortening
3/4 cup brown sugar, firmly packed
1 1/2 cups flour
1 egg
1 teaspoon salt
1/2 teaspoon baking soda
2 tablespoons water
1/2 cup chopped nuts
1 cup chocolate bits

Mix to the tune of *She'll Be Comin' Round the Mountain.*

Cream the shortening with the sugar, cream it well.
Stir the mixture with a spoon, now give a yell.
Add the flour to the bowl;
Add the egg as you are told.
Stir the mixture with a spoon and add the salt.

44

Mix the soda with the water, mix it well.
Add the mixture to the bowl, now give a yell.
Add the nuts and chocolate bits;
Stir as if you're having fits.
Stir the mixture in the bowl, as you are told.

Take a teaspoon of the mixture and be neat.
Drop it carefully upon a cookie sheet.
Now repeat until you clean up;
Bake the cookies till they brown up.
Bake the cookies till they brown up—fit to eat.

Bake 10 to 12 minutes. Makes 30 cookies.

Gold Star Oatmeal Cookies

Preheat oven to 350 degrees.

You will need: measuring cups, measuring spoons, stirring spoon, bowl, teaspoon, ungreased cookie sheet.

Ingredients:

1/2 cup shortening
1 cup brown sugar, firmly packed
1 teaspoon vanilla
1 egg
3/4 cup flour
1/2 teaspoon salt
1/2 teaspoon baking soda
1 1/2 cups rolled oats
1/4 cup chopped nuts

Prepare cookies to the tune of *The Red River Valley*.

If you cream well the shortening with the sugar,
If you add vanilla and egg, too,
If you mix in the flour, salt, and soda,
Then there's little left now to do.

If you add the oats and add the chopped nuts,
Stir it all with spoon and blend with care,
Drop by teaspoons on a sheet for baking,
You've earned the hat chefs proudly wear.

Bake 10 minutes. Makes 30 fat cookies.

Oh, My Darling Sugar Cookies

Preheat oven to 400 degrees.

You will need: bowl, stirring spoon, measuring cups, measuring spoons, teaspoon, lightly greased cookie sheet.

Ingredients:

1 cup brown sugar, firmly packed
1 cup soft butter
3 cups flour
1 1/2 teaspoons baking powder
1/2 teaspoon salt
1 egg, slightly beaten
3 tablespoons milk
1 teaspoon vanilla
1/4 cup sugar (to sprinkle over unbaked cookies)

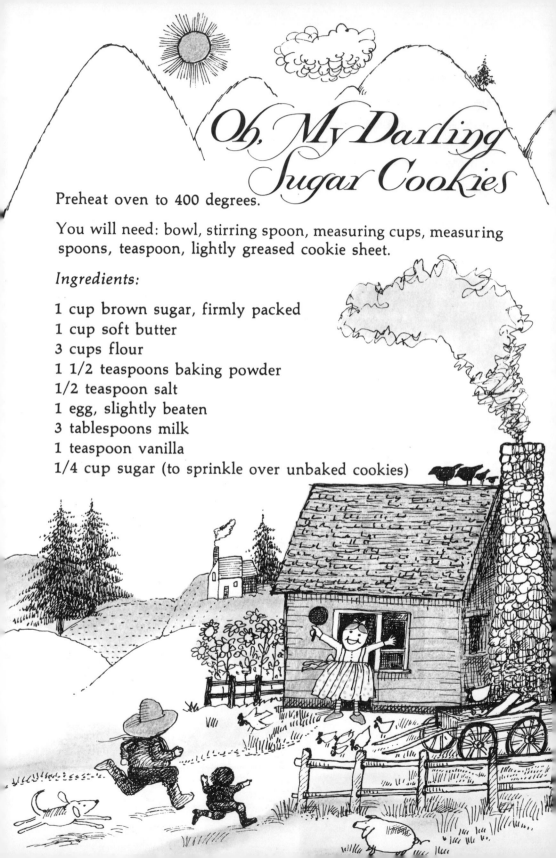

Mix in a bowl to the tune of *Clementine*.

Mash the butter with the sugar;
Stir it twenty times and then
Add the flour, baking powder;
Add the salt and stir again.

Add the egg and then the milk and
Add vanilla, if you please.
Stir and scrunch well with your fingers
Till you work the dough with ease.

Oh, my darling, Oh, my darling,
Sugar cookies, you are fun!
You will soon be in the oven,
In my tummy when you're done.

Wash your hands and with a teaspoon
Drop the dough on cookie sheet;
Flatten each drop with damp fingers;
Top with sugar for a treat.

Bake 5 to 8 minutes. Makes 4 dozen fat cookies.

Sugar Crumb Pies

Preheat oven to 350 degrees.

You will need: large bowl, measuring cups, measuring spoons, stirring spoon, 2 8-inch pie pans, clean fingers.

Ingredients:

2 cups flour
1 1/2 cups sugar
1/2 cup shortening
1 pinch salt
1/2 cup milk
2 eggs
2 teaspoons baking powder
1 teaspoon vanilla
1 teaspoon cinnamon sugar

In a bowl plop the first 4 ingredients. With clean fingers scrunch and squish until you've mixed everything together. Take out 1 cup of the scrunch—I mean, mixture—to use as topping later. Now please wash your hands again.

To the mixture left in the bowl, add the milk, the eggs (remove from shells first, please), the baking powder, and the vanilla. This time use a spoon instead of your fingers to scrunch and squish until the mixture is one big gloop.

Grease 2 pie pans and then divide the mixture (be fair) into the pans. Sprinkle 1/2 cup of the topping over each pie. Then sprinkle 1/2 teaspoon cinnamon sugar over each pie. (If you don't have cinnamon sugar, a bit of plain cinnamon will do.)

Bake for 45 minutes or until pies look done (but not done in). Keep one. Share one with your favorite neighbor.

Apple Doodle

Preheat oven to 350 degrees.

You will need: 1-quart buttered casserole dish, plastic bag (to crush crackers), measuring cups, measuring spoons, stirring spoon, bowl.

Ingredients:

8 cheese Ritz crackers, crushed
2 cups apples, peeled and chopped
1/4 teaspoon pumpkin spice
3/4 cup water
1 tablespoon lemon juice
1/4 cup brown sugar, firmly packed
2 tablespoons butter

52

Mix in a bowl to the tune of *Camptown Races*.

The crackers should be crushed up well. Doodah! Doodah!
But if they're not, no one will tell. Oh, doodah day!
    (Repeat same melody)
Mix apples with crushed crumbs and spice. Doodah! Doodah!
Add water, juice, and stir well twice. Oh, doodah day!

Pour in dish somehow. Sprinkle sugar now.
Oh, dot with butter and then bake away.
Apple Doodle-dah day!

Bake 40 minutes. Makes 3 servings. Top each serving with
vanilla ice cream.

Rainy Day Popcorn

You will need: measuring cups, measuring spoons, 3-quart pot with lid, large bowl, small skillet, stirring spoon.

Ingredients:

1/4 cup oil
1/2 cup popping corn
1 teaspoon salt
1/4 stick oleomargarine

Melt oleo in skillet on low heat and set aside.

Pop to the tune of *Old MacDonald Had a Farm.*

Put oil and corn into the pot.
E - I - E - I - O!
Cover pot and heat till hot.
E - I - E - I - O!
With a Pop! Pop! here, and a Pop! Pop! there.
Here a Pop! There a Pop! Everywhere a Pop! Pop!
Shake the pot; let popping stop.
E - I - E - I - Oooh . . . *Look how fluffy!*

Pour the popped corn into bowl.
E - I - E - I - O!
Salt and stir in oleo.
E - I - E - I - O!
With a Munch! Munch! here, and a Munch! Munch! there.
Here a Munch! There a Munch! Everybody Crunch! Crunch!
Popcorn, popcorn, down you go.
E - I - E - I - Oooh . . . *So delicious!*

Celery Snack

You will need: measuring cup, paring knife, measuring spoons.

Ingredients:

2 stalks crisp celery
1/4 cup crunchy peanut butter
2 tablespoons apple, chopped
2 cookies, crumbled
1 tablespoon milk

Wash celery stalks and remove tops. In a measuring cup, place remaining ingredients and mix well.

Make to the tune of *There's a Hole in the Bucket.*

There's a rut in the celery. Oh, gracious! Oh, golly!
There's a rut in the celery. Oh, what shall I do?
You shall fill it with stuffing, with stuffing you'll fill it.
You shall cut up the celery into smaller stalks, too.

With what shall I serve it? Oh, gracious! Oh, golly!
With what shall I serve it, the celery, with what?
Serve a good cup of cocoa, serve cocoa so jolly.
Serve cocoa with celery when you've filled up the rut.

With a crunch-crunch, sip, crunch-crunch. Oh, goodness! Excuse me!
With a sip-sip, crunch, sip-sip. Excuse me! Crunch-crunch!

To make cocoa, mix together in a cup: 1 tablespoon cocoa,
1 tablespoon sugar, and 1 tablespoon water. Stir well; then fill
up the rest of the cup with warm milk. Stir again and sip.
Serves 1 snacker.

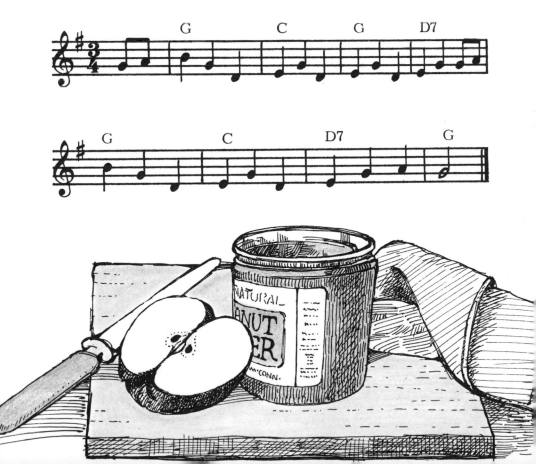

Party Sandwiches

You will need: 2 small bowls, stirring spoon, measuring cup, measuring spoons, chopping knife.

Ingredients:

1/4 cup celery, chopped
1/2 cup cooked chicken, diced
1/4 cup mayonnaise
2 tablespoons pecans, chopped
5 frozen slices of bread

Cut away crust and cut each slice of bread into 4 pieces to make 2 small sandwiches.

Mix in a small bowl to the tune of *Frog Went A-Courtin'*.

Chop up the chicken, celery too. Uh-huh!
Add the pecans; stir in mayonnaise. Uh-huh!
Make special sandwiches with this spread.
Garnish tops so they'll look well-bred.
Uh-huh, uh-huh, uh-huh!

To make garnish: Place 1 tablespoon of mayonnaise in a small bowl and add just 1 drop of red food coloring. Stir; then spread over sandwich tops. Add a sprinkle of dried parsley flakes and 2 shakes of paprika over each sandwich. Uh-huh!
Makes 10 party sandwiches.

Merry Holiday Berries

You will need: bowl, measuring cup, measuring spoons, stirring spoon, fork, clean hands.

Ingredients:

1 (3-oz.) package cream cheese
1 1/2 cups powdered sugar
1/2 teaspoon vanilla
5 drops red food coloring

(Set aside an extra 1/2 cup powdered sugar to add if the mixture ends up a little gushy.)

Mix to the tune of *Deck the Halls.*

Mash the cream cheese till it softens.
Fa la la la la, la la la la!
Mix it with the powdered sugar.
Fa la la la la, la la la la!
Add vanilla; add food color.
Fa la la, la la la, la la la!
Blend and shape into fat berries.
Fa la la la la, la la la la!

Roll the berries in red crystal sugar if you like. Makes 24 merry berries.

Celebration Punch

You will need: punch bowl with cups and ladle, large stirring spoon.

Ingredients:

1 pint lime sherbet
1 pint pineapple sherbet
1 quart cold ginger ale

Mix to the tune of *Auld Lang Syne.*

Scoop frozen sherbet into bowl
And shape into a crown;
Pour ginger ale against the sides
To keep the fizzing down.

For *Celebration Punch,* my dear,
Will make a party grand.
So stir it up and place a cup
Into each waiting hand.

Serves 10 to 12 happy ones.